The Museum of Unwearable Shoes

The Museum of Unwearable Shoes

Poems by

Gene Twaronite

Kelsay Books

Cover design: Shay Culligan

Library of Congress Control Number: 2018952980

ISBN: 978-1-949229-06-6

Kelsay Books
Aldrich Press
www.kelsaybooks.com

To *my* Josephine—not Hopper's—
who fills the "endless afternoon of now"

Praise for *The Museum of Unwearable Shoes:*

The Museum of Unwearable Shoes is simply stunning, filled with biting wit, subtle humor, insights, provocative questions and fresh looks at ordinary things that I'll never again experience in the same way. I love the way Twaronite peeks beneath the ordinary, leaving me moved and at times inspired by what he finds there. Even the few poems whose images and metaphors I find disturbing also provide insight in how to deal with such things. Reading this book was a wonderful adventure and I look forward to going back many times to again probe its depths.

Susan Lang, Faculty Emeritus at Yavapai College and author of the novels *The Sawtooth Complex* and *In God's Trailer Park* as well as a trilogy of novels about a woman homesteading in the southwestern wilderness during the years 1929 to 1941.

Acknowledgments

The author gratefully acknowledges the editors of the following print and online periodicals, where these poems first appeared:

Broad River Review: "Faith"

Ginosko Literary Journal: "A Would-Be Mix," "After Hearing the Young Black Poet," "Democracy at the Mall," "What the Gargoyle Sees," "Peeling the Bark"

The Ibis Head Review: "Trailing Words"

James Gunn's Ad Astra: "Journey to the Center of the Poem"

Lowestoft Chronicle: "The Museum of Unwearable Shoes"

New Myths: "The Next Big Thing"

Not One of Us: "Free Universe"

Parks & Points: "The Trail Back"

The RavensPerch: "Arguments at Eleven," "Deep Discount," "Droppings," "Feeling the Heat" "Pigeon Spikes" "Prescription," "Reading the Chaos," "Timepiece," "Whenever I See Empty"

Sandcutters: "A Blank Page," "Rehearsal," "Rejection"

Snowy Egret: "Pterodactylus"

Starline: "Letter from the Grave"

Tipton Poetry Journal: "All That Was Needed," "An Endless Afternoon of Now," "Message in a Body," "Rape and Shell Collecting," "Things Forgotten"

Tucson Weekly: "Captive Spaces"

Wilderness House Literary Review: "Answer Man," "Conversations," "The Last Fact," "The Stuff of Poetry"

Contents

A Blank Page

If I put a word here, say
for instance, extravagance,
how would that look? Or
if I gave it a whole line
e x t r a v a g a n c e
like something that fills
the sad space in your life
by pumping itself up
to seem important.

What if I put in a long pause...?
not because I need to,
but to make you stop and listen
for whatever comes next as if
the words held sacred truth.

What about all that space
along either side of this page?
  I could
  pull it in
  like so

or take it all the way out to the farthest reaches of space
just because it is there and I can.

Does it matter what I say here or how?
Do words depend on me to give them life
or do they possess lives of their own?
Do they rise and go to work each day,
and come home again to sleep at night?
Do they aspire to perform great things,
to come together with other words
in poems and speeches for the ages?

Maybe in the meantime I should
give them something to do,
some little task around this page
to make them feel useful.

And if I don't write something
to fill this void today,
would it be a tragedy
if I left it empty?

An Endless Afternoon of Now

*It wouldn't be bad to be that way, suspended in time—not bad at all, an
endless afternoon of now.*
                    —John Steinbeck, *The Winter of Our Discontent*

To enter you must first
choose a now—sitting
on a bench with your
first love and the touch
of her knee against yours
or the way you watched
him through the window
as the train pulled slowly
away from the station—
think of Hopper's
Josephine standing
naked to the dunes,
a cigarette dangling
from her fingers,
and you get the idea.
Make it something for
the ages, something
that looks good on the wall.

Message in a Body

When the radiance
of your face
leaves me blank,
when my bowels
evacuate
as they please,
when words
have no meaning,
you will know
it is time
that I go.
But if your time
comes first,
I will remember
your wish—
unlike mine—
from the way
you study so
curiously
the stranger
before you,
from the way
you struggle
to say what
your mind can
no longer think,
from the way
you stare
resolutely
at the future
as if to stab it
with your will
to hold a place
for you still.

Democracy at the Mall

Seems strange to talk of government by the people
in this corporate domain, where every move
is manipulated by apps and advertised needs
and the inescapable aroma of Cinnabon.

Yet, if you look past the dazzle and contrivance,
you will discover democracy alive and well
in this climate-controlled space,
where young families with their children
play in plastic playgrounds open to all,
where citizens in blue sequined outfits and coiffures
line up at the talent search for a shot at fame,
where dazed teens stare into their phones
seeking new parameters and connections,
where the huddled masses exercise
their inalienable right to shop
and promote the general welfare,
where a candy store promises *a piece of happy*
and another promises to *get your life in order*,
where you'll find Justice and domestic tranquility
and still Payless,
where there's *fashion for the people*
and you can vote for your favorite pants
(as long as it's *our* brand of pants),
where mall walkers can breathe the free air
finding sanctuary from weather's oppression,
where the people ordain this place each day
to secure the blessings of liberty
to themselves and their posterity.

Timepiece

For two weeks since my watch departed
I have scrutinized the skin of my left wrist
to see if my life is progressing.

What sequential madness demands I witness
each unfolding tick of my existence?

A new watch has appeared and my life is now digital
with no hands to point the way and no signs but
blinking numbers and a gentle chirp on every hour
reminding me to take heed of … what exactly?

Do we tack numbers on our lives to prove
we've passed from point A to point B
and to fill between the parentheses
in our obituaries?

Do the numbers measure real events—
a stream of moments as particles from the future
collide with the present to become the past?

Or is time all one piece—yesterday and tomorrow—
dancing cheek to cheek in eternal now?

When Tuesday Becomes Wednesday

Strange how one day
becomes another
and you slip into
a dimension so
real that you
begin to live there
oblivious to
the calendar
obeying only what
your mind believes
until the blinding
moment of impact
when you collide with
premature check-ins
titters and worried looks
as Tuesday comes calling.

Ode to Lucy

(On viewing Lucy, an *Australopithecus afarensis* fossil on display at Lucy's Legacy Exhibition, Houston Museum of Natural Science, 2007)

Who will I discover in my family tree?
Perhaps there's royalty in my blood,
some famous inventor or celebrity,
some brave soldier who died in the mud.

On a trip to Houston, I found my answer.
In a dim lit room, there you were—
your face budding like a dawn flower
from a branch of our chromosome tower.

Arrayed in glass-fronted coffin, your bones
burned into my vision like precious stones—
fragments of forearm, ribs, skull, and jaw
in the scant remains of you that I saw.

On one side is a model
of you staring back at me.
Like us, you walked upright,
bipedal, hands free.

Three-and-a-half feet tall you once stood,
with a pelvis that proved you were female.
If I could meet you in your ancient wood,
would you perceive me as a primate male?

Would there be some glimmer of recognition
from your apelike visage—a look of wonder
as if you've seen an apparition,
something from the world yonder?

.

Lucy, your grave robbers called you—
Lucy in the Sky—a fitting name
for someone who knew
how to play the survival game.

Though your brain was smaller than mine,
it was big enough for you and your clan
to last a hundred thousand years times nine—
far better than my human brand.

You had to grow up fast,
with little time for play.
Your challenges were vast
through the long night and day.

Unlike us, you were a swinger,
with strong arms and curved fingers,
who moved with grace and ease
on land and through the trees.

I would find it hard to live in a tree.
But perhaps living in two spaces
was your secret. Up there you could flee
your enemies as you sought out new places.

Forever I will see your face,
your strong jutting jaw and flat nose,
speaking to me from that honored place
in our family gallery with elegant pose.

Through your genetic wisdom
you taught us to climb high
while preparing our kingdom
on the ground nearby.

I see no blue blood or royalty
in that face, just your beautiful humanity
beaming back at me from beyond
across the eons.

There should be a constellation for you—
twinkling diamonds in the sky—
so that we may look up from our branch anew
and celebrate our family tie.

Peeling the Bark

As I drove past
the shirtless man,
his head wrapped
in cloth against
the desert sun,
he peeled the last
bit of bark
from a young
palo verde
as if to strip
away all
trace of green
from a world
he once knew.
How dare it grow
when acid hate
falls from the sky
and the ground
bears only fear
and despair,
when the buds
wither and die,
and the rot
goes all the way
to the roots.

Racism

The first syllable shouts
its name in your face as if
it were all that mattered.
Then its sibilant surname
cuts like scissors
the helical threads
that bind us.

The Last Fact

You might think it
one of those folks
like earth is round
or the sky is blue,
but those two died
years ago
in a rest home
where old facts go
to die in peace.
Everyone knows
earth is flat
and the sky any
color you want.
Like his parents—
death and old age—
he was stubborn
until the end,
hiding out in
dark taverns
of falsehood
and innuendo
drinking absinthe
to forget, but
forget he could not,
no more than
a forge can forget
what it fires,
or a sieve forget
what it filters.
Reality police
caught up one day
and brought him in
for questioning.
They beat the truth

out of him till
there was nothing left
but skin and bones
and a shiny red stain,
as the sun sank
in the east
and the stars shone
from the heavens
like distant campfires.

All That Was Needed

*All that was needed was an unending series of victories over
your own memory.*
                            —George Orwell, *Nineteen Eighty-Four*

Keep telling yourself
it never happened
wage relentless
assault on all
evidence to
the contrary
vanquish doubt
as you double down
on the message
memorize
then swallow
fix it firmly
like a favorite song
in the jukebox memory
of your hippocampus
play it again and again
as you reimagine the past.

Conversations

I don't mean to eavesdrop.
It's just someone's
always talking.
Did you hear about Marty?
He wasn't doin' nothin'—
just minding his own
business and they ...
I won't do it—
not this time.
I'm going to make
that bastard wish he ...
I try to ignore them,
but the words are like
open windows into
secret living rooms.
Sitting in the last row
on the Broadway bus,
I tell myself,
don't listen.
When someone nearby
starts up, I talk instead
to the person in my head.
Talk about what I plan to do
that night or where I'd go
if I had a zillion dollars.
Talk about great times
I've had or all the women
loved and gone,
which doesn't take long.
Talk about crimes
I didn't commit,
or those I didn't confess.
This is *my* life,
not someone else's.

Trouble is, I always want
to go through that window,
sit in a cozy chair
in the living room,
listen to someone new,
not my tired old self,
letting the words fall softly
on my ear as I nod knowingly,
holding out my glass
for another splash of wine.

Ground

It's that reassuring way
you force the tongue
against the roof of
the mouth and the low
drawn out pitch of
those two consonants
at the end that tell me
where to plant my feet.

Jade Plant on Lombard Street

A life moves
in turns and cross
purposes, like
the jade plant
that's supposed
to grow in a pot
inside a house
next to a window
looking out,
not a shrub
outside a house
on a street
switching
inside out
at every turn.

Mastermind

I saw the news on *CNN*—
Abdelhamid is dead—
and heard a voice inside me
rejoicing:
He is dead! He is dead!
His body mangled by bullets
and a nearby grenade,
he died not soon enough.
To call him mastermind
of the Paris massacre
makes him sound more
important than what he was—
just another cancer cell
in a metastasizing tumor.
Blind to everything but his belief,
he was master of nothing.
Relieved as I am to see
this murderous cell zapped
from the body of humanity,
I yet find myself looking back
at my thoughts, wondering
what kind of person it was
who could plot the deaths
of fellow humans as if
they were avatars
in a video game,
or whether he ever
looked up at the stars
and dreamed of a girl.
And I find myself wondering
what kind of mastermind it is
who this morning cheers

the death of a young man
who went so horribly wrong,
who once was human
before he blew it all up.

Hatemonger

You're a peddler
of prejudice in
a maggoty
marketplace
of vengeful lies
and ruined lives
where the only
currency is
fear.

What the Gargoyle Sees

You think it easy
leering down all day
with bestial gape
on the war below
as a widow cries
for a third son lost,
a one-eyed child
with half a face
stares up and smiles
at me before he dies.

To the Unknown Poet

Poets' Corner, Westminster Abbey

Here they lie, beneath the rose window
and the censing angels—Chaucer, Spenser,
Dryden, Browning, Tennyson, Masefield—
their words still soar through the vaulting spaces.
Even those buried elsewhere—
Milton, Keats, Burns, Blake,
Shelley, Eliot, Hopkins, Lear—
sing from the polished stones below.

And here you are as well
amidst the crush of tourists and the solemn weight
of so many tombs and monuments
to human greatness vying for attention.
With your spectacled, hungry young face,
hair neatly parted down the middle,
black coat artfully draped over one shoulder,
you cannot hide the poet yearning to be.
Passing slowly from stone to stone,
you gaze intently upon the chiseled names,
at times pausing and genuflecting
before your favorite sacred idols,
extending your fingers to the letters
as if to absorb
whatever power they may reveal.

Yours is not the hourly prayer of the priest on duty.
You reach out to another kind of creator,
seeking communion with voices from the past
and words that do not die
in hopes of discovering
truths still unknown to you.

May you find the inspiration you seek.
There is sweet music here.
Hear the blissful sound of these poets
and the fetal voice inside you.
Fear nothing, for, heart, thou shall find her.

Tis not too late to seek a newer world.
To strive, to seek, to find, and not to yield.
If every poem is an epitaph,
may your words be *tongued with fire.*
Sing thy songs of happy cheer.
Sit thee down and write in a book, that all may read.
Beauty is truth, truth beauty,—that is all
ye know on earth, and all ye need to know.

May you sail to the shores of Helicon
and drink from its fabled springs.
May you *weareth a runcible hat,*
and *dance by the light of the moon.*

(With quotations by William Blake, Robert Browning, Geoffrey Chaucer, T.S.
Eliot, Edward Lear, Percy Blysse Shelley, and Alfred, Lord Tennyson)

The Museum of Unwearable Shoes

The mall has many wonders
and most amazing of all is
the Museum of Unwearable Shoes
where perched on glass
pedestal displays of torture
you'll find multi-strapped
leather sculptures adorned
in beads and buckles
that bind and pinch
with exquisite agony
and six-inch gravity
defying dagger stilettoes
guaranteed to make
a woman look sexy—
except for bunions
and the moment her
face meets the earth.

Agony

You rhyme with peony
but unlike the flower
your bloom brings only
misery with your first
drawn-out syllable
that hangs in the air
like a hopeless cry.

Words to Heart

Who says I'm not their rightful owner?
They were mere words until I opened
my heart and gave them a home.
I call out their names in the dark
and they come frolicking
with new resonance and tricks.

Dearest is *absurd*—silly and preposterous,
but for me the bedrock of unreality,
from nonsense lines revealing hidden truths
to ruminations on things that should not be,

Which brings up *awe*, especially
when it whispers in my ear
at the sight of a Tyrannosaur skull
or the fossil light from a galaxy
billions of years in the past.

How I love to watch *moment* and *eternity*—
the way they play against each other
in their dance of continuity.
I try to catch them, but they're
always too fast, moments
merging with brothers and sisters
into eternity.

And when I grow weary of the daily strife—
there is always *nothing* to console me
with its noteless music and numbing
release from all being.

Faith

Faith is the bird that feels the light and sings when the dawn is still dark.
—Rabindranath Tagore

you call it.
I fear a bird
who sings
without reason.
Give me a bird
with clock
and compass
in her head
who sees
the dark
and knows
what it once was,
who sings in
celebration
of light's daily
resurrection
and the dawn
she knows
will come.

Belief

Like a loaded gun to the head,
you leave no room for debate,
but oh what comfort you bring
in times of fear and doubt—
just sit back and set controls
to automatic pilot.

Rape and Shell Collecting

A young teacher listened as his student shared her story—
which like all her stories he found impossible to classify—
told with the usual verve, drama and many-layered shells
of fact, fiction, truth, and beauty,
involving two neighborhood boys and the rape
of her friend in a world far beyond the classroom.

Watching her depart, he returned to his classroom,
dark and empty. Whatever he replied to her story
is forgotten. All he could hear was the word rape.
Tomorrow his students were to learn how to classify
in the language of science and, he hoped, to appreciate the beauty
on display in trays filled with brightly colored shells—

olives, whelks, augers, turkey wings, cockles, and tulip shells—
he had collected at Myrtle Beach to bring back to the classroom
to share with his students their intricate beauty
and a part of himself in the wondrous story
of their discovery while his students learned to classify,
but there was that word again—rape.

Why did it haunt him so? After all, it was not *her* rape
but her friend's. Yet now the shells
had lost their luster and become mere random objects to classify
in yet another sterile exercise in the classroom
with no connection to the human story,
no intrinsic beauty.

How could students like her appreciate the beauty
of nature's diversity against the brutality of rape
that should never be part of a thirteen-year-old's story
yet there it was, calcifying year by year into hardened shells
to block out memories from life's ugly classroom
of events and things they cannot classify.

How could he expect them to appreciate and classify
objects when they could not appreciate their own terrible beauty?
He expected them to sit and learn in the classroom
when they came to him with lives inconceivable where rape
shatters hopes and dreams like storm-tossed shells
and making it through another day is the only story.

But classify they did, next day, as the teacher shared his story
in the classroom bathed with morning sunshine where rape
was banished … and a woman recalls the beauty of colored shells.

Rehearsal

Of all I have owned—
mountain view cabin
two quaint houses
acres of woodlands
with mossy boulders
and hidden brooks
gardens I planted
left for someone new
books and treasures
collected over a lifetime
red MGB of my youth
Plymouth van of middle age
Toyotas of autumn—
the best part
lay in leaving them.

Whatever pleasure I derived
was quickly forgotten
in the moment of release.
Only then did I know
the perverse satisfaction
of letting go.

Possessions still come
then depart with no regret.
Each time is a rehearsal.
No longer bound to my fancy
I am once again free—
one step closer to a self
unencumbered by holding
one step closer to leaving.

Friends

For three nonstop hours
they talk
consuming the other's
words and thoughts
as if osmotically
through a mutual membrane
insults flying between them
like buzzing bees
gently stinging each other
in sweet ecstasy.

Backing Out

Shifting into reverse is what I do best.
You could call it a vocation.
Sometimes out is in and east is west.

Leaving jobs or relations is no big test.
Whatever the occasion,
shifting into reverse is what I do best.

Promise the sky and the moon and all the rest,
just leave me my rationalization.
Sometimes out is in and east is west.

The few things in life I haven't messed
up are my only consolation.
Shifting into reverse is what I do best.

Precious survivors, they must be blest
to resist annihilation.
Sometimes out is in and east is west.

That anything remains I never would have guessed,
for whom the only way forward is extrication.
Shifting into reverse is what I do best.
Sometimes out is in and east is west.

Sublime

Your name gives you away
with the first breath that
surfaces are not your game
nor where the treasures lie,
but deep below in that
last humming rhapsody.

Trailing Words

What happens
to words when
the listener
moves off before
you've finished?
Do they try
to follow
like faithful
homing pigeons
delivering
their message?

Who hears them
after they launch
from your lips
in fervent
discussion
trailing behind
you on their own
down the sidewalk
murmuring
on the wind
making new lives
for themselves?

What do they do
when we speak
into empty rooms
then remember
and close the door?

Do they linger
respectfully
for a while
in bittersweet
mourning of
words unheard?

The Trail Back

is never the same.
The sun you once faced
is now over your shoulder,
the horizon where you're
headed is now the one
where you've been.
You follow your footprints
as you explore the world
made new in hindsight
hoping to find what it is
you have missed.

Things Forgotten

There's a store in the mall selling
personalized gifts engraved
to remember every occasion.
Too bad there's not a store
to help you forget
those moments
engraved on your brain:
that time in second grade
when the bully won and you ran away,
the slap in your daughter's face
and the slam of the door when she left,
the thud of his head as it hit the windshield,
the look in your wife's eyes
when she caught you in your naked deceit,
the words that still echo in your head
or the words you should have said,
the relentless pain she endured
that helped you decide at the end,
the hour just before dawn when you
relive the horrors again and again.
No need for engraving—sandpaper
and a buffing wheel will do,
applied judiciously to remove
just enough letters to dull the pain
without losing their meaning,
just enough to let you sleep at night.

Letter from the Grave

Just like him to wait till now—
always the procrastinator
promising to write but
never getting around to it.
I can barely read the words,
scrawled like drunken
worms across the page.
And look at that stationery,
all crumpled and rotted
like he didn't give a damn.
But what really ticks me off
is the postage due.

Rejection

As you digest the second rejection today—
no, you did not win the Topeka
chapbook prize, not even close,
and those poems held so long
by *Boston Review* ended up
"not right for us at this time"—
you might think your odds
of achieving literary fame
are roughly the same
as winning a Powerball ticket.
But still you wrote, polished,
submitted your manuscript
for a stranger to read
if only briefly before tossing it
into the pile of lost words—
words that you alone
had the guts to share.
You did not put your head
in the oven today.
You did not seek sanctuary
in drugs or booze,
at least not before noon.
Nor did you compose
an anonymous review of your work
praising "a new rising talent"—
though it might not hurt.
Maybe one day—
don't get your hopes up—
a reader will find your poem
and smile or cry
over a line you wrote
about what it means
to live and die.

So wear your crown of rejection
proudly this morning
as you write your new
obituary.

Prescription

Whenever I despair
I pop two words
in my mouth
then swallow.
They don't do
much at first—
it's like they're
waiting to see
how hopeless
I've become
to decide which
will dissolve,
laughter or
suicide.

Captive Spaces

Walking past city gardens
locked within their fences,
I see my old friends—
plants and buildings
who once reached out to me,
now safe from those
who would defile them.
Soaring spaces
dreamed by architects,
living landscapes
designed to bring
our desert closer—
their arms outstretched
through cold steel bars
as if clutching at the sky—
now held like convicts
in the prisons of our
failed imagination.

Feeling the Heat

Glacier National Park

On the far shore of Lake McDonald
their black stubble rises from the ridges
in stark reproof of fairytale forests
where trees never burn and die
lodgepole pine cones never open
bugs never burrow in wood
to feed the birds and grizzlies
scorched trunks and limbs
never break and turn to dust ...
smoke from a dozen wildfires now
burning outside the park remind me
to smell death with every breath
to feel the heat of combustion
that sustains and consumes us.

Seven Lessons

Here on the edge of what we know, in contact with the ocean of the unknown, shines the mystery and beauty of the world.
—Carlo Rovelli, *Seven Brief Lessons on Physics*

I.

Physicist or poet, we plumb
the depths of our existence.
We sail through space-time—
not pulled, but falling—
swirling like leaves
into its curved embrace.

II.

The world is not what it seems.
The light tracks through the window
like a train of particle passengers,
leaping between compartments,
popping in or out of existence
as they collide in mutual chaos,
defying prediction of where
or when they will appear,
only the probability
that they will.

III.

The world grows smaller
as the sky grows larger.
Once there was only
earth below and sky above.
Then the sky reached outward
to become a celestial sphere.
Reluctantly the earth

59

relinquished its throne
to the sun—now a star—
taking its humble place
among the planets.
No longer could the sun
boast of its proud family,
as other stars revealed
solar systems of their own.
And the Milky Way
gave up its milk
to a hundred billion stars,
just one in a curving sea
of countless galaxies
moving through the cosmos
on waves of time and space
born from a hot dense speck.

IV.

The smaller the world grows,
the further we see.
Much of it lies hidden,
viewed only through a dark lens.
Atoms split to divulge
finer particles still,
constantly appearing
then disappearing,
buzzing and humming in their
restless quantum dance.
The void is not empty,
but an endless state of being
and non-being on the way
to becoming something else.
Fluctuation is the only reality.

V.

The world is not things,
but rings of space
woven together from
a fabric of relationships—
a marriage of space and matter
dancing to the music of gravity.

VI.

The world is more probable
than not, so it exists.
Nothing happens except by chance.
We live by the laws of heat
in a world of imaginary time.
Each moment seethes with potential.
We dream up existence,
choosing which moments
to observe in the present
and which to file in the past,
while the future is already here.
We live in a black hole
whose horizons we cannot see.

VII.

We are inside and outside,
indivisible.
The neurons in our brains,
like stars in a galaxy,
send out their signals,
yet shine not apart but
with the integrated light

of a hundred billion suns.
We are each a system
of thought and feeling,
creating the reality we see.
Poets paint the world in words,
swirling strands of life into meaning.
Physicists paint the world in data,
tracking the footprints of phenomena.
Both drink from the same dark fountain,
the source of all wonder and truth.

Writing in the Multiverse

I know you're there—
a slight stir in the air,
a shift in possibility
to another reality.

I don't know who you are.
Maybe you live inside a star
or exist as a being wrought
out of pure thought.

Anyway, just thought I'd say hello
to an alternate writer fellow.

The Stuff of Poetry

Give them circles of Hell
the stench of battlefields
and young lives lost
love's passionate embrace
a young mother's grief
at her stillborn child
the vanity and futility
of all endeavor
despair that falls
like acid rain
doubt and faith
the ways we meet death
and off they go
writing verse that matters.

But give them something
like a hangnail
or the place you
always stub your toe
the fit of your new sneakers
that little lift you get
when your favorite tune
plays on the radio
or the cute way
you still pull in your gut
when a young girl passes by
the quiet sigh you make
every morning
for no particular reason…
and their voices go mute
as if there's nothing
sacred or profound
no truth or beauty
in life's detritus.

Pterodactylus

Replicated in resin
above my reading chair
your limbs and clawed
wings seem poised to
vault from the cliff and
soar over Jurassic seas.

Crestless head and tiny
body reveal you were
new to the game
but with wings unfurled
no boundary could
stop you as you
followed your prey
into a denser world.

I see the flickering
spark from your eyeless
sockets as your still weak
muscles struggled to
take off again to
keep your head
above the waves.

At last you sank into
soft sediments below where
bones became stone and
reality met immortality.*

*A recent hypothesis to explain the prevalence of juvenile pterosaurs in the
fossil record suggests that they might have died from drowning.

Evolution

You start out simply
with two short sounds
but the way you shout
that third syllable
leaves no doubt you're
the kind who likes
to shake things up
and start something new.

Droppings

The wayward poem goes where it will,
yanking me in unknown directions,
snuffling its big wet nose
where I fear to tread.

I yell for it to stop, but it
runs on down the lines
before I can catch a breath,
chasing rabbit thoughts
to dubious conclusion.

Where did I lose control?
Should I send it to obedience school?
Teach it to heel and do tricks
like other poems do,
fetch the paper and sit
faithfully by my side.
But I know too well.
it would rather run free,
fur flying, with
tricks of its own.
Play dead Lazarus
back from the grave.
Pretend it's a being
of pure form.
Or imagine it's
a hot tiny particle—
where are you, Spot?—
expanding into a universe.

Who am I kidding?
I will follow
wherever it takes me
through dusky forests

of forgotten memory
and beyond.
Maybe someday I
will learn its tricks.
For now all I can do
is watch in wonder
as the master
races through the trees
snuffling the dead leaves,
breathing them into life.
Then off it goes
howling in ecstasy.
I track its prints
in the damp earth.
But all I find
are its droppings
fresh on the trail,
as if left to remind me
how I came to this last line.

Canyon Stories

James House, Ramsey Canyon

The way it sets into the south-facing slope above the floodplain
the way its faded boards softly weather in the sun
make it blend into the natural scene
like a fallen tree
a gentle reminder of settlers' brief reign.

But in the setting sun long shadows
of their rough ways still linger ...
blasting a toll road through the canyon
to build their mining camp
with dance hall and saloons

channeling the creek into twisted contortions
and narrow channels to water their orchards
while choking out riparian trees
hunting the wildlife
while ignoring the richness of its diversity

slashing oak, pine, and fir from the mountaintops
to graze their livestock while suppressing cool fires
that swept the forest floor of small trees and debris
scouring the slopes of their minerals while seeding
what's left with false claims and when it is all spent
leaving the hillside to its barren solitude.

Sycamores, oaks, and junipers now press
against the rotting walls where spiny lizards dwell.
Visitors with binoculars take only what they see.
The wind blows clean through the forest
and the creek flows free again.

When Lizard Eyes Meet Mine

Squiggle of sunshine
poised for flight
eyes blazing
back at me
inscrutably
across the eons.
Do you see
only danger
or can you see
my eyes light
up looking
out to yours
searching for
a connection?

Journey to the Center of the Poem

To Jules Verne

Dare I follow the cryptic runes of Saknussemm,
descending into the shadow-kissed crater
seeking unknown tunnels to the center?

Why undertake a journey
so inconvenient or improbable?

One does not need to climb
a volcano in Iceland to find
pathways worthy of exploration.

Indeed, why journey at all
and not let Life come to us
in prepackaged servings?

And what's so great about a point
equidistant from the ends?
Surely there are plenty of things
to be found in the prelude—
those first few tentative steps in the darkness
when the enormity of your task
fills the heart with dread and you
wish you'd never left home.

But, tired and thirsty, you plug on
through the arid lonely tunnels
until realizing you're hopelessly lost.

And let us not forget the finale.
Isn't getting there what really counts?
Just tell me how it ends.

Did they meet their fate bravely?
Did they finally escape?
Did the love birds get married?
And was there some purpose to it all?

But the poem knows otherwise.
Only in the center will you find
subterranean caverns bathed in strange light,
vast oceans teeming with sea monsters,
forests filled with petrified trees, mastodons,
man-apes, and other creatures from your past.

There you must come to terms
with whatever perils lie in wait
around the next bend.

No one can save you from yourself.
It will all end here, lost and forgotten
in the bowels of an unexplored world,
or you'll take the journey to its conclusion,
your raft swept by the rushing waters
into the volcano's chimney,
carried on a rising surge of magma
by the primal heat of creation—
up, up, up until ejected in elation
into the clear blue sky above Stromboli.

Free Universe

It was a nice space
as universes go—
everything was free there,
from love, will, and time
to lunch, radicals and verse.
But the cost was too dear,
it could not last,
as even the strong force
was freed of its role
and things flew apart.
They had a big sale
but no one came,
so they closed their doors
and blinked goodnight.

Arguments at Eleven

It's like some shock jock station
broadcast directly to my head
devoted solely to arguments
from a past that never ends.

I'll be brushing my teeth
or staring at the alarm clock
when the show comes on
forcing me to tune in:
the clash with high school classmate
still strident across the years
though he's long since dead;
the raging battle with my brother
three Thanksgivings ago
that I'll never win;
the red-faced shouting
matches with my dad
spinning round and round
for paternal eternity.

The best shows come late
at night with guest appearances
by people I don't even know
challenging me to defend
some point I hold dear.

It matters little what they say,
my words drown them out—
dripping with eloquence
too late as if I'm still
prepping for debate.
Wish I could turn it off,
but that's the price you pay
for 24-7 entertainment.

Answer Man

You have an answer for everything,
my dad would say, with a wry stare
at his smartass son.

He never tired of the mantra,
invoking it as a shield
against my college boy erudition.

All he had to do was name
an issue and an answer
would pop from my head

like Athena, fully formed
out of the skull of Zeus,
invincible in her armor.

I wish we could talk again,
to tell him the armor has rusted
and the answer man is gone

along with his
glib solutions
to all life's problems.

All I have left is a river of data
flowing like Lethe through
an underworld of unknowing.

Dipping my net into dark waters,
I capture some slower-moving bits
and examine them under a microscope

to see if there's any pattern
or philosophy to them,
some way to grab hold.

And just when I think I've found
a plausible interpretation
for their behavior,

a storm surge of new data
sweeps away all my hypotheses
and grand theories,

leaving me right back
where I started, skimming
the waters of my ignorance.

Insubordination

There's something about
the tone of your voice—
all those syllables
with their accusatory
accents judging without
asking why, demanding
only that I comply.

After Hearing the Young Black Poet

speak, my first reactions were
sadness, rage, then wonder
at our different worlds—
he writes of the bullet
he knows has his name on it
while I write—again—of my
imminent decrepitude,
he writes of all the times
he was stopped and frisked
while I write of indignities
suffered at airport security,
he writes of how his
great-great-great grandfather
was sold and branded like cattle
while I write of how my
Lithuanian grandfather's name
got butchered at Ellis Island,
he writes of how it felt
to watch the first black president
compared to a monkey
while I write of how
my big ears always turned red
whenever kids laughed at them,
he writes of the pain
that won't go away after
seeing his son killed because
a policeman felt threatened
while I write of the day
a policeman's wife shot her husband
dead in the bedroom above us

and I felt sad for my poor dad
cleaning bits of brain off the walls,
he writes knowing that for some
he will always be less of a man
while I write whole and secure.

We explore the separate
flows of our lives, holding
them back against time,
diving for words
in quiet pools of reflection,
but it's a wonder
his dam doesn't burst.

A Would-Be Mix

is what I am,
wishing my skin
were some other shade
than Baltic white.
Would that my identity
were forged in strife
rather than immunity.
Would that my genes
could express all
the colors I lack.
Would that my heart
could know what it
feels like to be
ignored, beaten, raped,
jailed or excluded
because I'm not
one of them.
Would that the bittersweet
mysteries of my
brothers and sisters
were mine and I could
check off the box marked
all of the above.

They Planted Ocotillos Where the Homeless
Used to Pee

What once was a quiet corner outside the library
where sleepover patrons could pee in obscurity
will soon become a wall of spiny stems, hostile
to squatting humans and bared appendages.
A place once stained by stinking waste
will sprout new green leaves with every rain,
crimson flowers in spring and summer,
where you don't have to hold your nose
as you walk down the sidewalk or
turn your head away except maybe
in shame because a barrier garden
is the best we could do.

Dumbfounded

You've always known that
the first rule of sanity
is to remain silent in
the face of absurdity.

People You Meet Along the Wash

Santa Cruz River Park, Tucson

What street is that way?
asks the woman
emerging from the shade.
Congress Street, I tell her.
So that's north? she asks.
No, that's south, I reply,
giving her a lesson in
directions whether
she wants one or not
starting with where
the sun rises
and watch her face
while the information
sinks in and fades.
What street is that way?
Congress Street, I say,
then resume my walk
as she stands
and stares south.

A young man dangles
an empty wrapper
over the iron fence
as I pass, then throws
it into the wash.
He turns as if in
reply to whatever
I might be thinking.
There's a coyote
down there. I'm feeding
him part of my sandwich.
I nod and smile.
Yes, I've seen them too.

But as I continue along
the wash it occurs to me
not once have I ever shared
my sandwich with a coyote.

Reading the Chaos

Our selves, refound in the world, are what we respond to, feeling outward things as part of us.
　　　　　　　　—Damion Searls, *The Inkblots: Hermann Rorschach, His Iconic Test, and the Power of Seeing*

I cannot escape them
the woman's profile
in the bathroom tile
the paint-textured
demon on the wall
the shifting shapes
that darkness takes,
the coded messages
in words received
the structures I build
each day to hold reality
images projected
onto everything I see
the Martian face
that isn't there.
Would that I could see
beyond the patterns
to live without certainty
reading the chaos
between the lines.

Whenever I See Empty

I seek to fill it
whether it needs filling or not
inserting my vanity into spaces
undefiled by actuality
as if I could fill the vacuum
between the stars and electrons
as if I could fill the gulf between us
no matter how close you seem
as if I could fill your vacant stare
so you don't have to be there alone
as if I could fill all the holes
and lonely places within me
as if I could fill the blank slate
with words enough to keep the void at bay.

Atmosphere

With your first high note
you lift me up into
that ethereal world
you call home as you
envelop me with
a round sweet sound
like the breath of Earth.

The Next Big Thing

Think I'll pass on
self-driving cars
and wait till
someone invents
a self-driving
me so I can
surpass myself
doing a hundred
and ninety
and eat my dust.

Abyss

Like an image in a book
that frightened you as a child
and always made you slam
the covers shut until next time
you opened it and there it was
waiting to terrorize your eyes
on that which can't be,
it's still deep inside you—
look below—see the bottomless
hole of its hungry mouth.

Where Words Go to Die

Born from a womb of cerebrum and culture,
words live out their lives, then die.
They are neither baptized nor confirmed,
though a few are consecrated
in great speeches on fields of battle
and shall not perish from the earth.

Most words live modestly
just trying to be useful,
like *you* and *I, he she it* or *is*.
They don't call attention to themselves.
Maybe that's the secret to long life.

Other words flare up briefly,
igniting conversation with their
fun sounds and meanings, then burn out
leaving only ashes and chiseled names
in the graveyards of once popular media.

There was *gumfiate*, all puffed up with pride,
and *kexy*, who ended up dry and withered,
not to mention *lardlet*, the little piece
of bacon who gave so much to meat.
Great *woundikins*! Their spirits
still murmur on the wind.

You can tell when words are about to go
by who uses them. You don't hear young folks
saying *bunkum* when they mean nonsense.
It's a pity *gallivant* has grown old and feeble—
oh, the pleasures we shared on the road.

Some words grow old from overuse—
awesome, incredible, and *unbelievable*
as it sounds, and don't get me started on *unique*,
who used to be such a nice, one-of-a-kind word.

Often it's technology that shows words the door.
The world looked so bright for *floppy disk*.
Now he can't get a job anywhere,
except in government.

All words, from the moment
first uttered by their creator,
have an inalienable right
to life, however long,
and a death with dignity.
There should be some quiet place, a hospice
where words go to die.
Soft music would lightly play, as they
gaze at the garden through the window
chatting goodbyes to friends on Facebook,
making their final peace with the world.

In Memoriam

There will come a moment
when other neurons have
failed and you alone will be
left to turn out the lights.
Whoever you are, I
ask one favor—that you
think of me and drink a toast
to our last flash and all
the good times we shared.

About the Author

Gene Twaronite is a Tucson poet and author of seven books, including two juvenile fantasy novels and two short story collections. His first collection of poetry *Trash Picker on Mars* was published in 2016 by Aldrich Press (Kelsay Books imprint), and was the winner of the 2017 New Mexico-Arizona Book Award for Arizona poetry.

Follow more of his writing @ www.thetwaronitezone.com.